Just the Opposite

Big
Small

Sharon Gordon

MARSHALL CAVENDISH
NEW YORK

My bed is big.

Your bed is small.

My dog is big.

Your dog is small.

My bus is big.

Your bus is small.

My bike is big.

Your bike is small.

My horse is big.

Your horse is small.

My present is big.

Your present is small.

My ice cream is big.

Your ice cream is small.

My bubble is big.

Your bubble is small.

Pop!

19

Words We Know

bed

bike

bubble

bus

20

dog

horse

ice cream

present

21

Index

Page numbers in **boldface** are illustrations.

About the Author

Sharon Gordon has written many books for young children. She has also worked as an editor. Sharon and her husband Bruce have three children, Douglas, Katie, and Laura, and one spoiled pooch, Samantha. They live in Midland Park, New Jersey.

With thanks to Nanci Vargus, Ed.D.
and Beth Walker Gambro, reading consultants

Benchmark Books
Marshall Cavendish
99 White Plains Road
Tarrytown, New York 10591-9001
www.marshallcavendish.com

Library of Congress Cataloging-in-Publication Data

Gordon, Sharon.
Big small / by Sharon Gordon.
p. cm. — (Bookworms: Just the opposite)
Summary: Two siblings compare the sizes of things they are familiar with, from the buses they ride to the beds they sleep in.
ISBN 0-7614-1568-8
1. Size perception—Juvenile literature. 2. Size judgement—Juvenile literature. [1. Size.] I. Title. II. Series: Gordon, Sharon. Bookworms. Just the opposite.

BF299.S5G67 2003
153.7'52—dc21
2003004525

Photo Research by Anne Burns Images

Cover Photos by Jay Mallin

The photographs in this book are used with permission and through the courtesy of:
Jay Mallin: pp. 1, 2, 3, 4, 5, 8, 9, 10, 11, 12, 13, 14, 15, 16, 17, 18, 19, 20 (top) (bottom left), 21.
Corbis: p. 6 Tom Stewart; pp. 7, 20 (bottom right) Tom & Dee Ann McCarthy.

Series design by Becky Terhune

Printed in Malaysia
3   5   6   4   2